LIGHTNING BOLT BOOKS™

Do You Know about Fish?

Buffy Silverman

Lerner Publications Company
Minneapolis

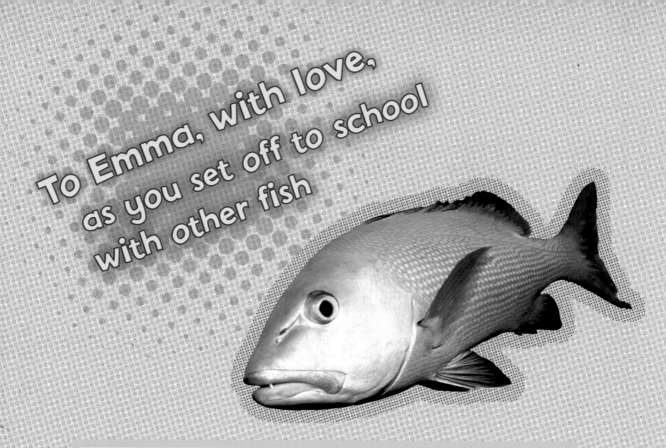

To Emma, with love, as you set off to school with other fish

Lerner Publications Company
A division of Lerner Publishing Group, Inc.
241 First Avenue North
Minneapolis, MN 55401 U.S.A.

Website address: www.lernerbooks.com

Library of Congress Cataloging-in-Publication Data

Silverman, Buffy.
        Do you know about fish? / by Buffy Silverman.
            p.   cm. — (Lightning bolt books™—Meet the animal groups)
        Includes bibliographical references and index.
        ISBN 978–0–8225–7540–5 (lib. bdg. : alk. paper) 1. Fishes—Juvenile literature. I. Title.
        QL617.2.S57 2010
        597—dc22   2008048904

Manufactured in the United States of America
1 2 3 4 5 6 — BP — 15 14 13 12 11 10

Contents

All Shapes and Sizes

Fish live in water. They swim in ponds, streams, lakes, and oceans.

Fish come in all shapes and sizes. Some are huge. Whale sharks grow longer than your classroom. Others are tiny. Goby fish are smaller than a coin.

Goby fish are tiny.

Fish swim in the warm Indian Ocean.

Most fish cannot make their own body heat. Fish warm up or cool down with the water they live in. This kind of animal is called an ectotherm.

Fish: Inside and Out

Fish are shaped for slipping through water. They wave their tails to swim. Sailfish have long tails. Their tails help sailfish speed underwater.

Sailfish travel as fast as cars on the highway.

Most fish have fins. Fins on the top and bottom keep a fish from rolling over. Pairs of fins on the sides of a fish's body help it steer.

This shark has fins on its tail, back, and sides.

Fins help fish move through the water. Fish use their fins to turn and stop.

The lionfish's fins look like a lion's mane.

Many fish are covered with scales.
Hard scales protect their skin.

This picture shows a
salmon's scales close up.
Scales fit together like
shingles on a roof.

A shark's scales look like tiny teeth. All the scales point toward the shark's tail. That helps the shark slip through the water as it swims.

These are scales on a dogfish shark.

A porcupine fish puffs up
when it is in danger.

Watch out for its pointy scales!

Can you feel bones in your back? **Fish have backbones too. Animals with backbones are called vertebrates.**

Can you see this tetra fish's backbone?

The whale shark is the world's largest fish. Like other fish, its backbone runs from its head to its tail.

The backbone is part of a fish's skeleton. The skeleton gives a fish its shape.

Like you, fish must breathe. But fish breathe in water. A fish breathes with its gills. A fish opens its mouth. Water flows in. It closes its mouth, pushing water over its gills. That way, a fish gets oxygen from water.

You can see gills inside this fish's mouth.

14

Fish have small openings on the sides of their heads. Water passes over the gills and then goes out of these openings. In fish like sharks, these openings are called gill slits.

A lemon shark has five gill slits on each side of its head.

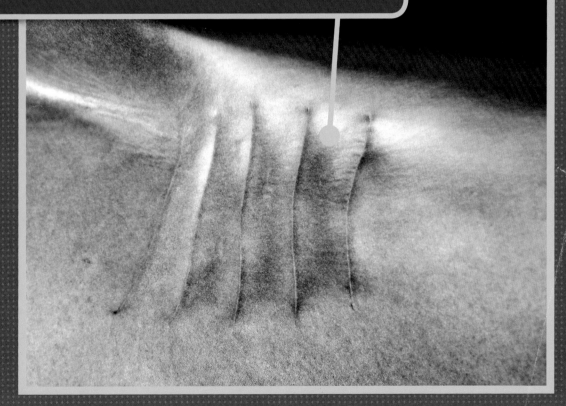

Fish look for food on a coral reef.

Staying Safe

Many animals eat fish. But fish know when other animals swim near them. They have tubes along the outsides of their bodies. The tubes are called lateral lines. They help fish sense moving water. The tubes help fish keep away from danger.

This fish has a stripe along its lateral line.

Some fish stay safe by helping big fish. Cleaner fish swim inside a grouper's mouth. Will the grouper swallow them?

Cleaner fish swim around a grouper's mouth.

No! Cleaner fish eat food that is trapped between the grouper's teeth.

Some fish blend with their surroundings. Seahorses match seaweed and floating plants. They rest and hide on these plants.

Do you see a seahorse?

Anchovies swim in groups, called schools. They are safer in groups.

There are hundreds of anchovies in this school.

An Amazon leaf fish looks like a floating leaf. Larger fish do not bother it. Smaller fish swim close. Then the leaf fish gulps a meal.

A leaf fish stays safe because other animals mistake it for a leaf.

Baby Fish

Most fish lay eggs. Baby fish hatch from the eggs. A sunfish lays 300 million eggs at a time. Many of the eggs get eaten by sharks and other fish.

Can you see baby fish in these eggs?

Rays grow egg cases to protect their eggs. Baby rays grow inside the hard cases.

This hard case holds a ray egg. Thin strings hold the egg case to a piece of coral.

A male stickleback builds a nest. The female lays eggs in it. The male guards the eggs to keep them safe.

A male stickleback carries a snail away from his nest.

Cichlid fish carry eggs in their mouths. After hatching, the babies swim into their mother's mouth when there is danger.

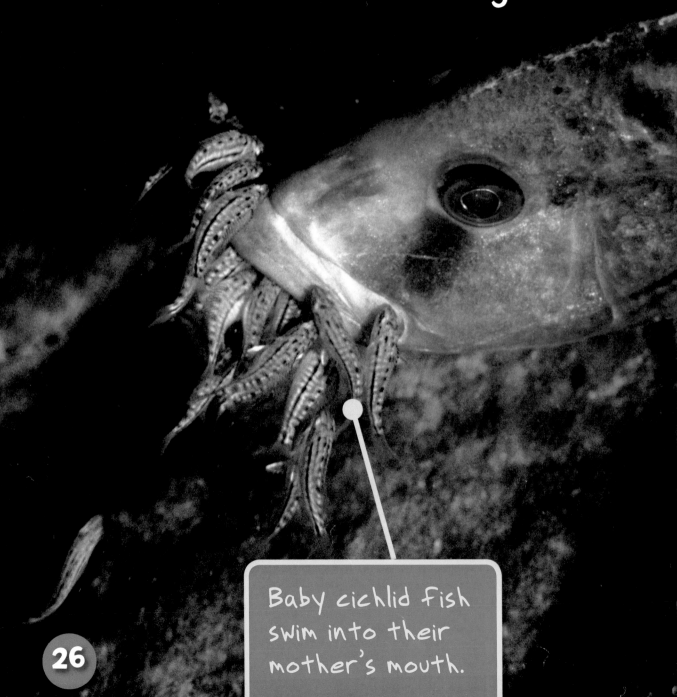

Baby cichlid fish swim into their mother's mouth.

Guppies don't lay eggs. They
give birth to baby guppy fish.
The babies breathe, swim, and
eat in their watery home.

This female guppy will
have babies soon.

Weird and Wonderful Fish

Blind cavefish have no eyes. They live in caves where there is no light. They find their way by using their lateral lines.

This blind cavefish uses senses other than sight to find its way.

Electric eels can make electricity. While hunting, they stun their prey with an electric shock. They also use electricity to find and choose mates.

Seahorse dads give birth to baby seahorses. A female seahorse puts her eggs in her mate's pouch. He carries the eggs until they hatch.

Mudskippers can "skip" across a muddy swamp. They walk on their fins.

This male seahorse is holding eggs in its pouch.

Glossary

ectotherm: a cold-blooded animal. An ectotherm's body warms up or cools down with its surroundings.

egg cases: hard bags that protect fish eggs

electricity: a form of energy that is found in nature or can be made in a power plant

fins: thin organs on the outside of fish used for swimming, turning, and balance

gills: organs in a fish that take in oxygen from water. Fish breathe with their gills.

lateral line: organ in a fish that helps it sense water movement

oxygen: a gas in air and water. Plants and animals need oxygen to breathe.

scales: small, thin, hard, flat plates that cover and protect a fish's skin

school: a large group of fish

skeleton: the framework of bones in an animal's body. The skeleton gives an animal its shape.

vertebrates: animals with a backbone. Amphibians, birds, fish, mammals, and reptiles are vertebrates.

Further Reading

Aquarium of the Pacific
http://www.aquariumofpacific.org/

Fish: National Geographic Kids
http://www3.nationalgeographic.com/animals/fish.html

Ichthyology at the Florida Museum of Natural History: Just for Kids
http://www.flmnh.ufl.edu/fish/Kids/kids.htm

Pfeffer, Wendy. *What's It Like to Be a Fish?* New York: HarperCollins, 1996.

Schleichert, Elizabeth. *Fish.* Washington, DC: National Geographic Nature Library, 1997.

Shedd: The World's Aquarium
http://www.sheddaquarium.org

Index

Photo Acknowledgments

The images in this book are used with the permission of: © Brian J. Skerry/National Geographic/Getty Images, p. 1; © Mark Conlin/Alamy, p. 2; © David Fleetham/Alamy, p. 4; © age fotostock/SuperStock, pp. 5, 13, 15, 17, 24; © Jeff Rotman/naturepl.com, p. 6; © Mark Carwardine/naturepl.com, p. 7; © Christopher Crowley/Visuals Unlimited, Inc., p. 8; © Paul Nicklen/National Geographic/Getty Images, p. 9; © Dr. Dennis Kunkel/Visuals Unlimited/Getty Images, p. 10; © Pacific Stock/SuperStock, p. 11; © Don Farrall/Digital Vision/Getty Images, p. 12; © Marty Snyderman/Visuals Unlimited, Inc., pp. 14, 18; © Image Source/Getty Images, p. 16; © Georgette Douwma/naturepl.com, p. 19; © Bill Curtsinger/National Geographic/Getty Images, pp. 20, 26; © Ken Lucas/Visuals Unlimited, Inc., p. 21; © Reinhard Dirscherl/Visuals Unlimited, Inc., p. 22; © Willem Kolvoort/naturepl.com, p. 23; © Kim Taylor/naturepl.com, p. 25; © Maximilian Weinzierl/Alamy, p. 27; © Ken Lucas/Visuals Unlimited/Getty Images, p. 28; © Paul Zahl/National Geographic/Getty Images, p. 29; © Medioimages/Photodisc/Getty Images, p. 30; © Daniel Gotshall/Visuals Unlimited, Inc., p. 31.

Front Cover: © Bill Schaefer/Getty Images (top); © Armando F. Jenik/The Image Bank/Getty Images (bottom); © Michael Aw/Lonely Planet Images/Getty Images (inset bottom)